What Would You Do with a Database?

Susan Kralovansky

Consulting Editor, Diane Craig, M.A./Reading Specialist

visit us at www.abdopublishing.com

Published by ABDO Publishing Company, a division of ABDO, P.O. Box 398166, Minneapolis, Minnesota 55439.

Printed in the United States of America, North Mankato, Minnesota
102012
012013

PRINTED ON RECYCLED PAPER

Editor: Liz Salzmann
Content Developer: Nancy Tuminelly
Cover and Interior Design and Production: Kelly Doudna, Mighty Media, Inc.
Photo Credits: Shutterstock

Library of Congress Cataloging-in-Publication Data

Kralovansky, Susan.
What would you do with a database? / Susan Kralovansky.
p. cm. -- (Library resources)
ISBN 978-1-61783-603-9
1. Internet searching--Juvenile literature. I. Title.
025--dc15

2012946826

Super SandCastle™ books are created by a team of professional educators, reading specialists, and content developers around five essential components—phonemic awareness, phonics, vocabulary, text comprehension, and fluency—to assist young readers as they develop reading skills and strategies and increase their general knowledge. All books are written, reviewed, and leveled for guided reading, early reading intervention, and Accelerated Reader® programs for use in shared, guided, and independent reading and writing activities to support a balanced approach to literacy instruction.

Contents

What would you do with a database?

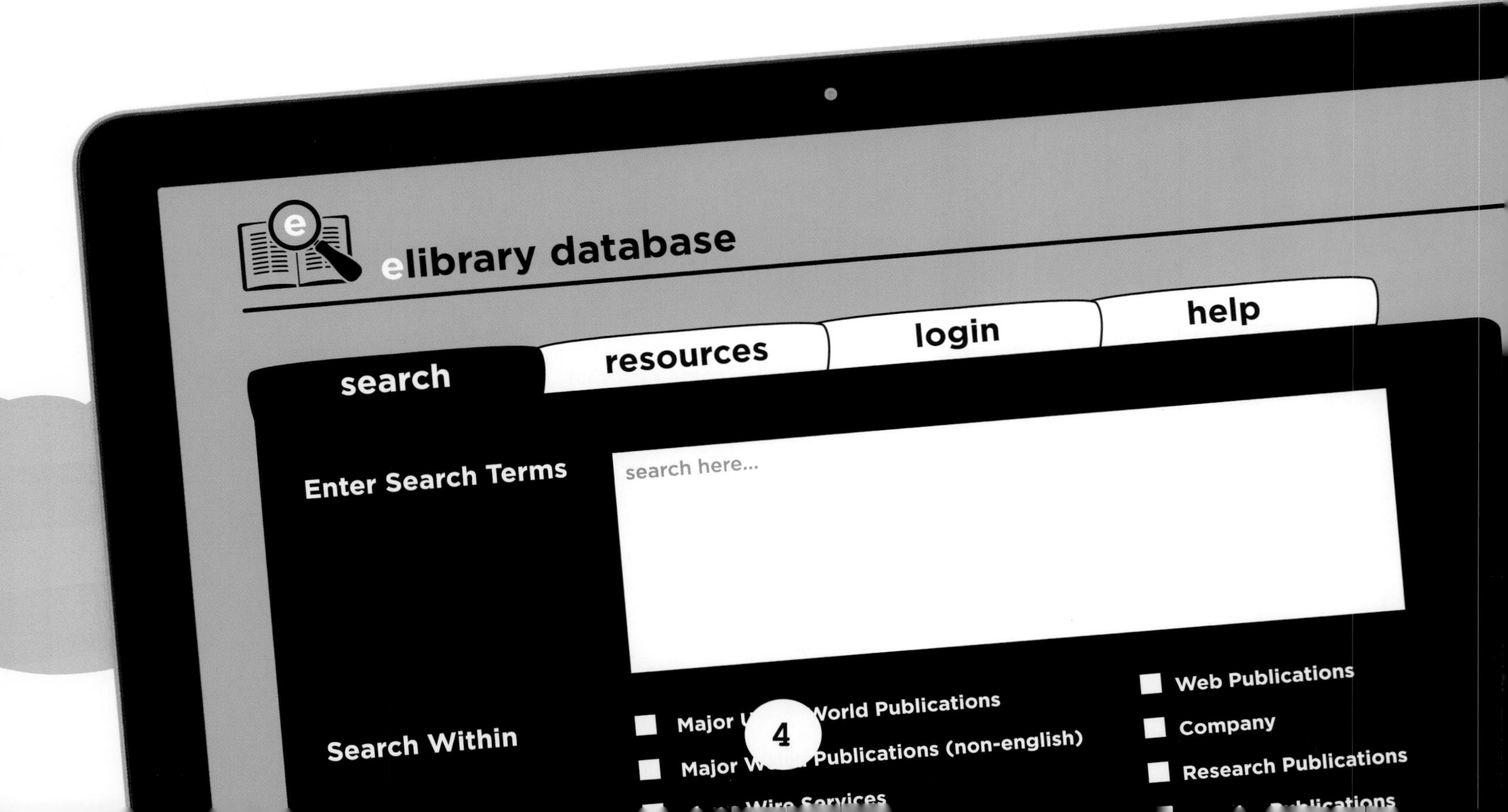

If you had a database you could look up anything!

The Database

A database is a library without walls. It has information about everything, anytime you want!

Most libraries have a Web page just for kids. Look for databases there.

To use a database you need a computer. Most databases are on the Internet. You may need a school I.D. or library card to use some databases.

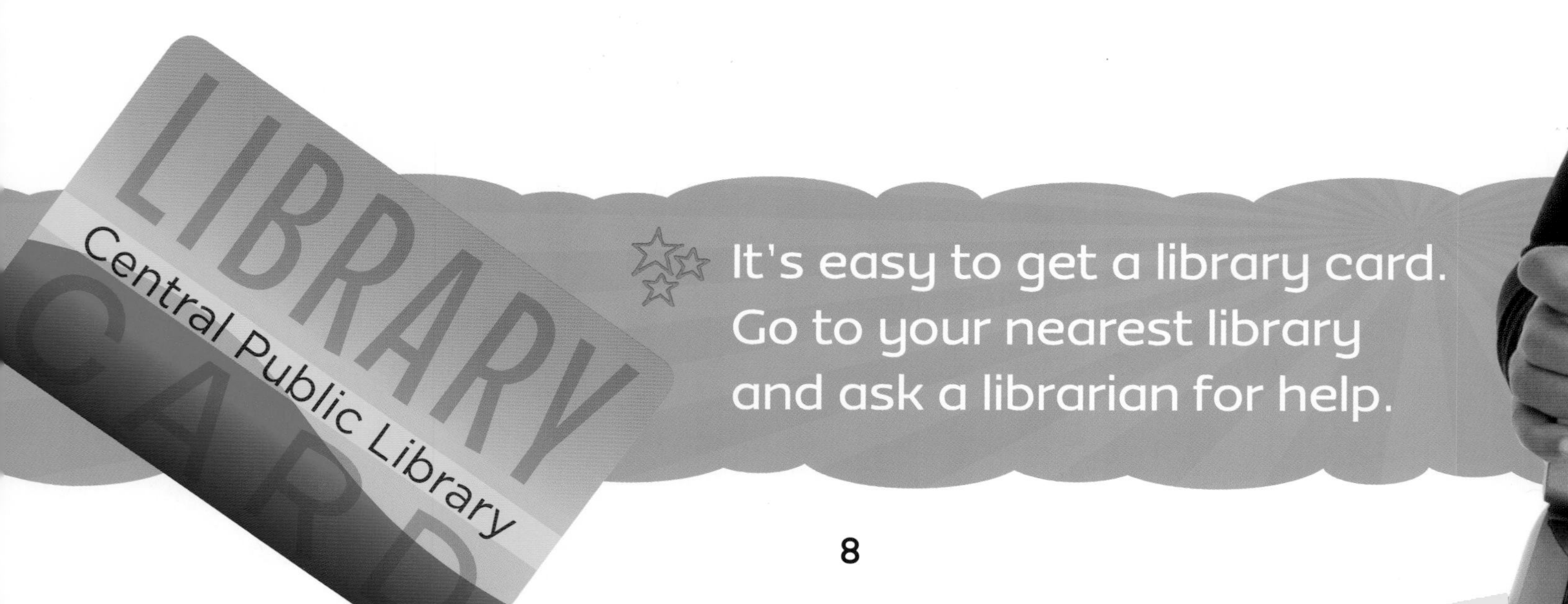

It's easy to get a library card. Go to your nearest library and ask a librarian for help.

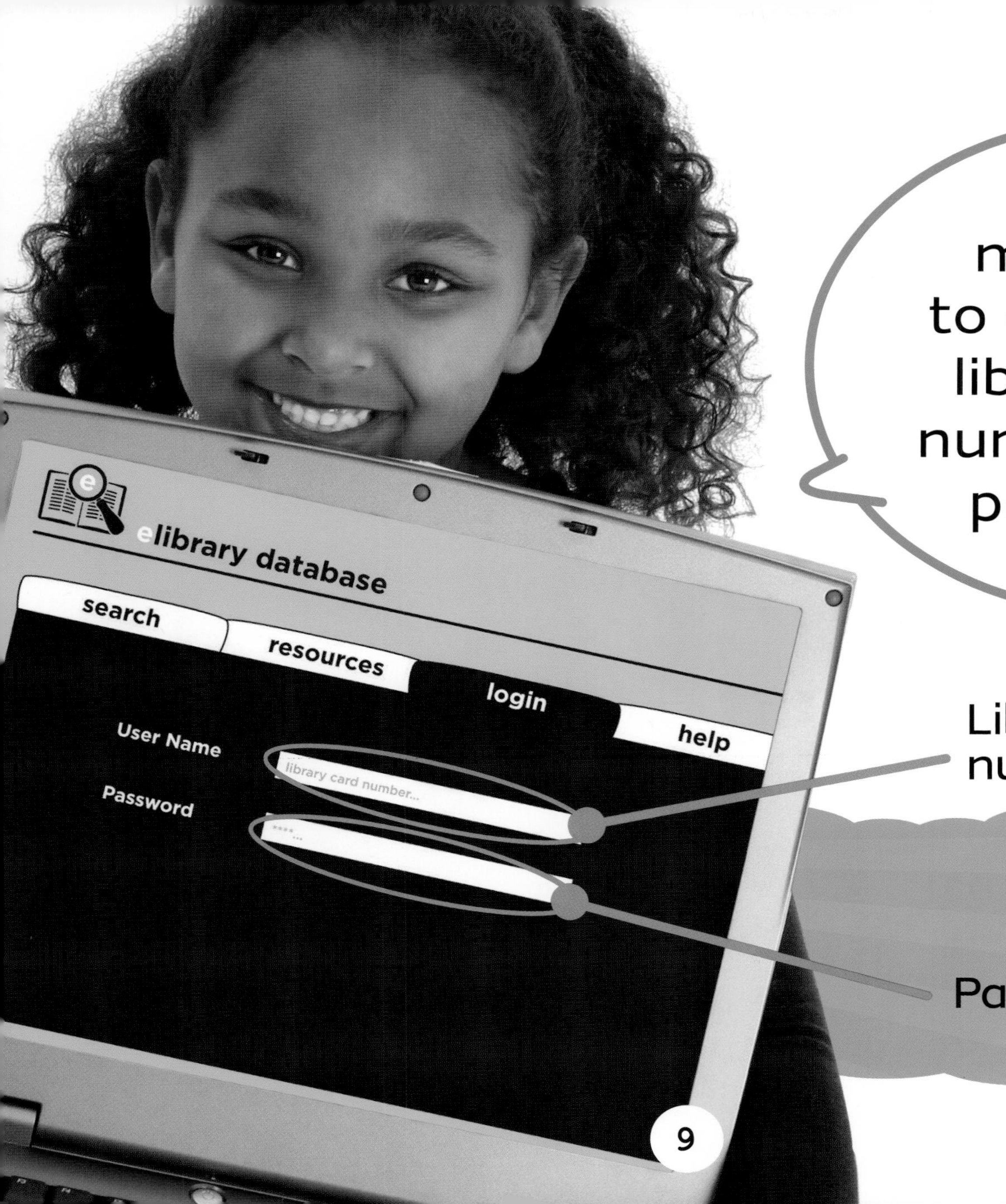

You may need to enter your library card number and a password.

Library card number

Password

Why not just look stuff up on the Internet? It's faster.

Surfing the Internet is not always faster or better. It is like asking for homework help from strangers. A database is a safer place to find information.

Before databases people searched for information using an index. It was written on paper cards.

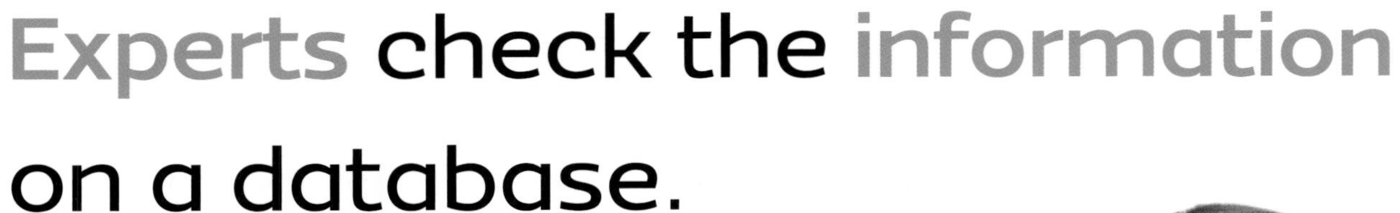

Experts check the information on a database.

It's easy to find information you can trust.

Picking a Topic

To use a database, you need a topic to search for. Try asking a question.

What about "How tall is a giraffe?" or "How much does an elephant weigh?"

That's a good place to start. A database is the perfect place to find answers to your questions.

I'm doing a report on Thomas Edison. My teacher says I have to find out all this information!

So, I have a topic. Now what do I do?
What did he do to become famous?
When was he born?
Where did he live?
Thomas Edison

Using a Database

There will be a *Search* or *Find* field. Type in a topic, such as "Thomas Edison."

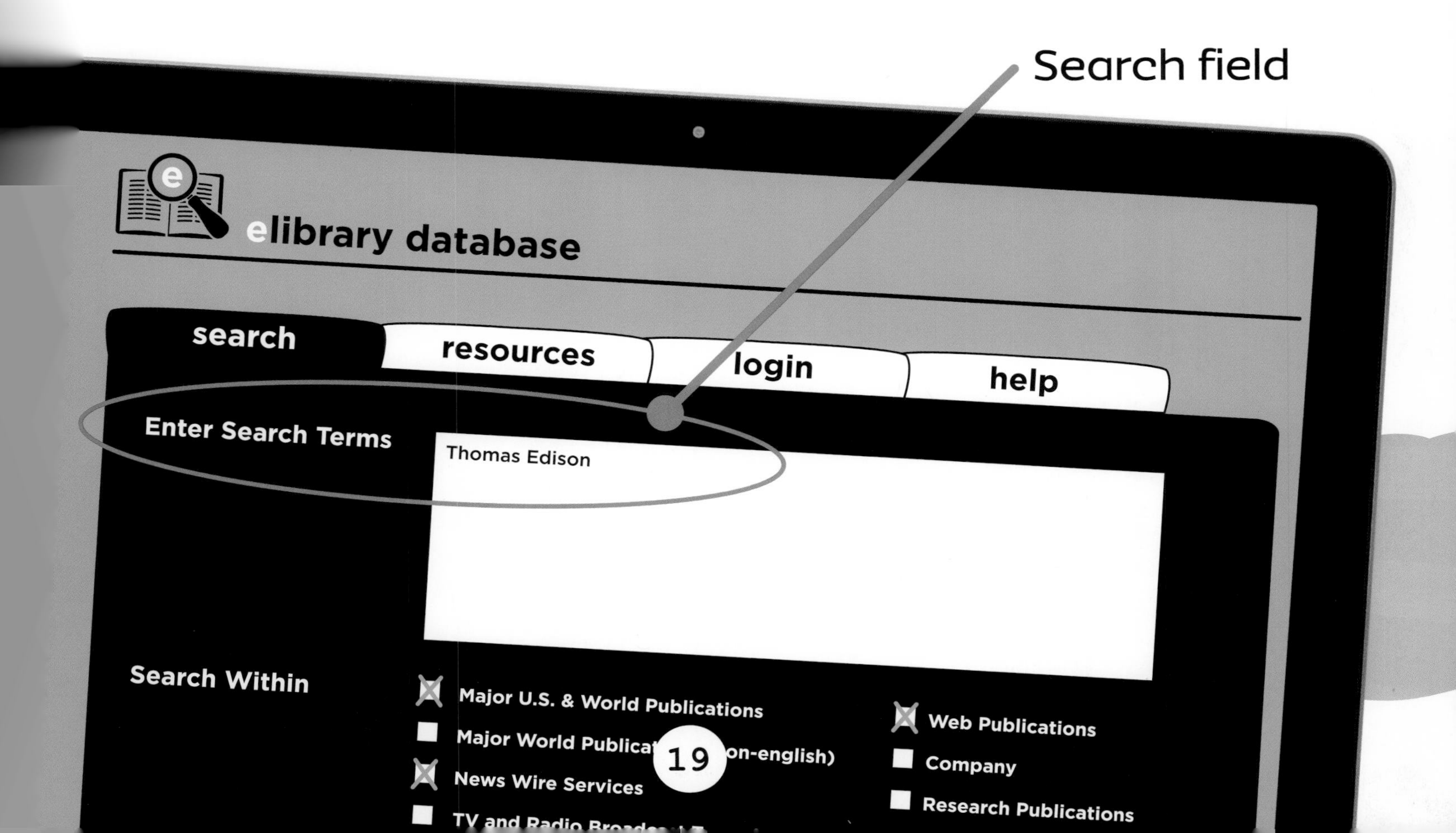

A list of results will pop up. They could be articles from encyclopedias, newspapers, or magazines. Just click on a title to read the article.

Use databases for homework or fun! You can learn a lot of things.

elibrary database

search

resources

Results for "Thomas Edison"

Encyclopedia Results

Thomas Edison - World Encyclopedia Article

Newspaper Results

A Short History of Light - The Daily Telegraph

Magazine Results

The Brilliance of Edison - Lighting Today

What if the database says it can't find anything for my topic?
elibrary
search
Enter Search Terms
search

If you get confused, click the Help link. It will lead you to an **expert** who can help you.

When you find what you want, you can print, save or email your information.

The first database for the Internet was created in 1989. It was called Archie.

More About Databases

Use a database to discover fun facts.

I learned about a guy named Evel Knievel. He was the first **extreme sport athlete**. He jumped over rattlesnakes and buses and sharks with his motorcycle!

If I use a database, will I still need books?

A database is one way to find information. Books are another. A good researcher uses both!

Conclusion

With a database you have a quick and easy way to find answers to your questions.

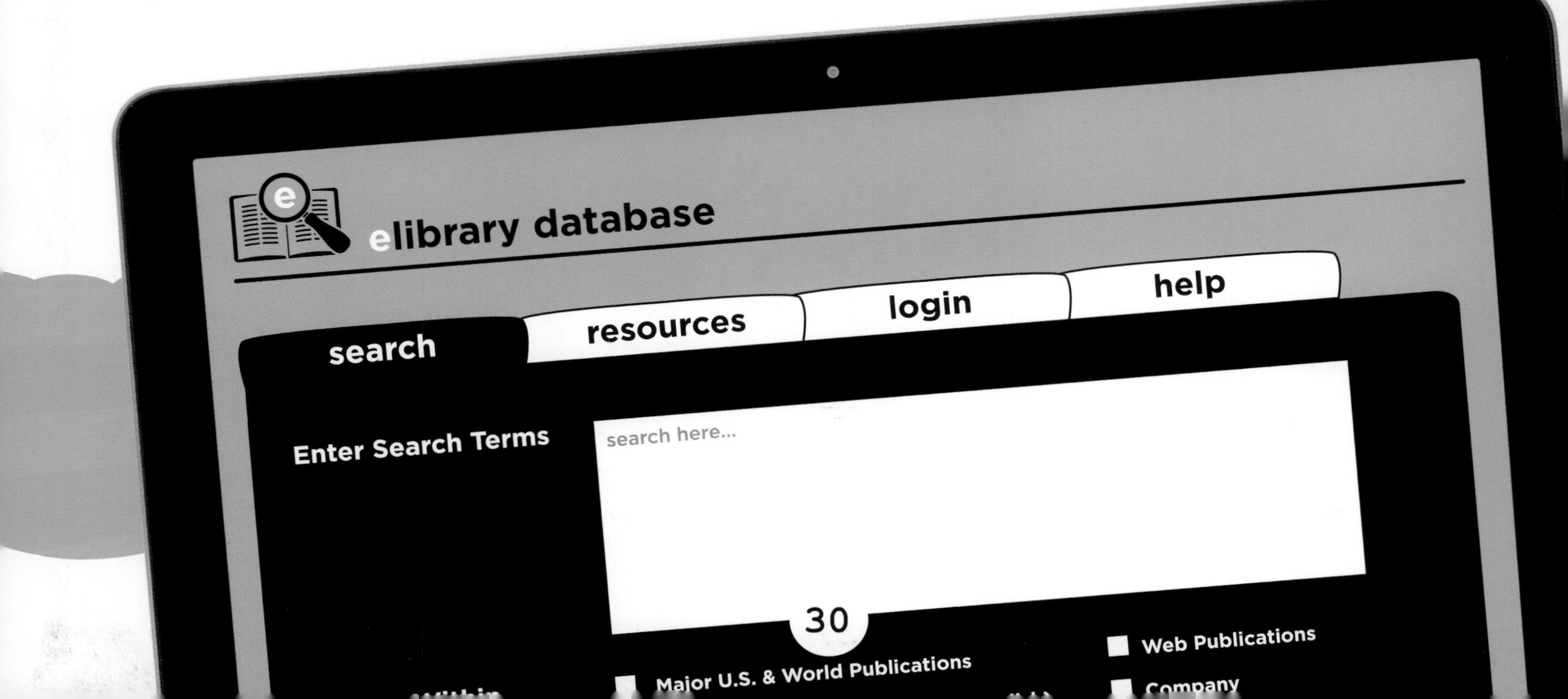

Glossary

athlete – someone who is good at sports or games that require strength, speed, or agility.

encyclopedia – a book or set of books with information arranged alphabetically by subject.

expert – a person very knowledgeable about a certain subject.

extreme sport – an often dangerous activity done for fun or competition, such as BMX racing or hang gliding.

information – something known about an event or subject.

researcher – someone who tries to find out more about something.

topic – the main idea or subject.